SACRED ROOTS

FRAMES
BARNA GROUP

SACRED ROOTS

Why the Church Still Matters

JON TYSON
RE/FRAME BY RICH VILLODAS

ZONDERVAN

Sacred Roots
Copyright © 2013 by by Barna Group

This title is also available as a Zondervan ebook.
Visit www.zondervan.com/ebooks.

This title is also available in a Zondervan audio edition.
Visit www.zondervan.fm.

Requests for information should be addressed to:

Zondervan, *Grand Rapids, Michigan 49530*

ISBN 978-0-310-43323-1 (softcover)

Published in association with the literary agency of The Fedd Agency, Inc,
401 Ranch Road 620 South, Suite 350c, Austin, TX 78734.

Cover design and interior graphics: Amy Duty
Interior design: Kate Mulvaney

Printed in the United States of America

13 14 15 16 17 18 /DCI/ 18 17 16 15 14 13 12 11 10 9 8 7 6 5 4 3 2 1

CONTENTS

....

WHY YOU NEED FRAMES

....

These days, you probably find yourself with less time than ever.

Everything seems like it's moving at a faster pace— except your ability to keep up.

Somehow, you are weighed down with more obligations than you have ever had before.

Life feels more complicated. More complex.

If you're like most people, you probably have lots of questions about how to live a life that matters. You feel as though you have more to learn than can possibly be learned. But with smaller chunks of time and more sources of information than ever before, where can you turn for real insight and livable wisdom?

Barna Group has produced this series to examine the complicated issues of life and to help you live more meaningfully. We call it FRAMES—like a good set of eyeglasses that help you see the world more clearly ... or a work of art perfectly hung that invites you to look more closely ... or a building's skeleton, the part that is most essential to its structure.

The FRAMES Season 1 collection provides thoughtful and concise, data-driven and visually appealing insights for anyone who wants a more faith-driven and fulfilling life. In each FRAME we couple new cultural analysis from our team at Barna with an essay from leading voices in the field, providing information and ideas for you to digest in a more easily consumed number of words.

After all, it's a fast-paced world, full of words and images vying for your attention. Most of us have a number of half-read or "read someday" books on our shelves. But each FRAME aims to give you the essential information and real-life application behind one of today's most crucial trends in less than one-quarter the length of most books. These are big ideas in small books — designed so you truly can read less but know more. And the infographics and ideas in this FRAME are intended for share-ability. So read it, then find someone to "frame" with these ideas, and keep the conversation going (see "Share This Frame" on page 84).

Furthermore, each FRAME brings a distinctly Christian point of view to today's trends. In times of uncertainty, people look for guides. And we believe the Christian community is trying to make sense of the dramatic social changes happening around us.

Over the past thirty years, Barna Group has built a reputation as a trusted analyst of religion and culture. We offer cultural discernment for the Christian community by thoughtful analysts who care enough to tell the truth about what's really happening in today's society.

So sit back, but not for long. With FRAMES we invite you to read less and know more.

DAVID KINNAMAN
FRAMES, executive producer
president / Barna Group

ROXANNE STONE
FRAMES, general editor
vice president / Barna Group

Learn more at www.barnaframes.com.

F R A M E S

TITLE	20 and Something	Becoming Home	Fighting for Peace	Greater Expectations
PURPOSE	Have the Time of Your Life (And Figure It All Out Too)	Adoption, Foster Care, and Mentoring – Living Out God's Heart for Orphans	Your Role in a Culture Too Comfortable with Violence	Succeed (and Stay Sane) in an On-Demand, All-Access, Always-On Age
AUTHOR	David H. Kim	Jedd Medefind	Carol Howard Merritt & Tyler Wigg-Stevenson	Claire Diaz-Ortiz
KEY TREND	27% of young adults have clear goals for the next 5 years	62% of Americans believe Christians have a responsibility to adopt	47% of adults say they're less comfortable with violence than 10 years ago	42% of people are unhappy with their work/ life balance

PERFECT FOR SMALL GROUP DISCUSSION

FRAMES Season 1: DVD
FRAMES Season 1: The Complete
　　　　　　　　　Collection

READ LESS.
KNOW MORE.

The Hyperlinked Life	Multi-Careering	Sacred Roots	Schools in Crisis	Wonder Women
Live with Wisdom in an Age of Information Overload	Do Work that Matters at Every Stage of Your Journey	Why Church Still Matters	They Need Your Help (Whether You Have Kids or Not)	Navigating the Challenges of Motherhood, Career, and Identity
Jun Young & David Kinnaman	Bob Goff	Jon Tyson	Nicole Baker Fulgham	Kate Harris
71% of adults admit they're overwhelmed by information	75% of adults are looking for ways to live a more meaningful life	51% of people don't think it's important to attend church	46% of Americans say public schools are worse than 5 years ago	72% of women say they're stressed

#BarnaFrames

www.barnaframes.com

Barna Group

 ZONDERVAN®

BEFORE YOU READ

....

- Do you think it's important to attend a local church? Why or why not?

- What do you find most compelling about church — either your church or church in general?

- What bothers you most about church?

- Overall, would you say the people you know — friends, co-workers, family members — have a generally positive or negative perception of the church? Why?

- What do you think is the purpose of the local church? Can you articulate a mission statement in summary?

- Do you think churches you know are accomplishing that mission? Why or why not?

- If the churches disappeared from your neighborhood or city, in what ways would they be missed — or would they?

SACRED ROOTS

Why the Church Still Matters

INFOGRAPHICS

13%
My kids learn about God there

8%
Does good work in the world

What do you think OF CHURCH?

About one-third of Americans say going to church is important, about one-third think it isn't important at all, and the rest of Americans fall somewhere in the middle. However, while people's opinions on church might be fairly evenly split, their reasons for loving or hating – or being indifferent to – church come in a wide variety.

- Those who say church is very or somewhat important
- Those who say church is not too or not at all important
- Millennials

5%
Friends are there

35%
Not personally relevant

10%
Not allowed to doubt

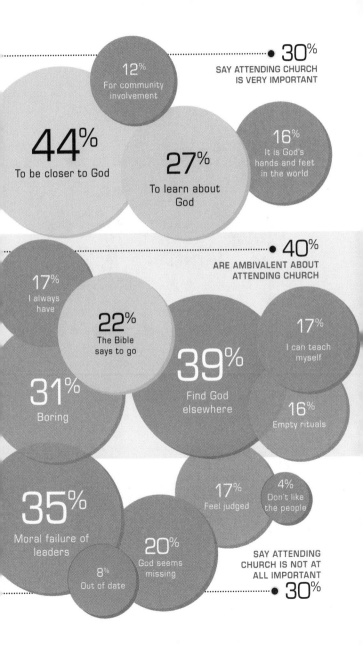

30%
SAY ATTENDING CHURCH
IS VERY IMPORTANT

12%
For community
involvement

44%
To be closer to God

27%
To learn about
God

16%
It is God's
hands and feet
in the world

40%
ARE AMBIVALENT ABOUT
ATTENDING CHURCH

17%
I always
have

22%
The Bible
says to go

17%
I can teach
myself

31%
Boring

39%
Find God
elsewhere

16%
Empty rituals

35%
Moral failure of
leaders

8%
Out of date

20%
God seems
missing

17%
Feel judged

4%
Don't like
the people

SAY ATTENDING
CHURCH IS NOT AT
ALL IMPORTANT
30%

Do you go to CHURCH?

Have attended church in the past week

When asked if they went to church in the past week, about four in 10 Americans say "yes." While that number hasn't changed dramatically in the past decade, it has trended downward slightly.

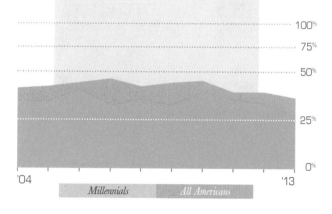

100%
75%
50%
25%
0%

'04   '13

Millennials   *All Americans*

59% of Millennials who grew up in the church have dropped out at some point

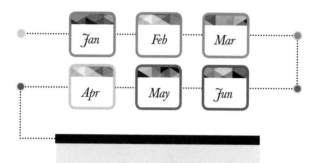

Have not attended in the past six months

The number of people who say they have not attended a church function at all in the past six months has increased considerably in the past 10 years. This is true particularly among younger Americans; more than half of Millennials haven't been to church in at least six months.

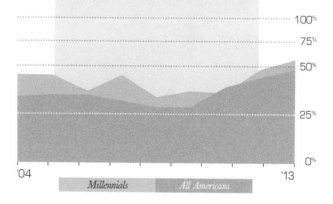

SACRED ROOTS

Why the Church Still Matters

FRAMEWORK

BY BARNA GROUP

Welcome to the post-religious age—where the once clean-cut ideas about faith and Christianity are breaking down. Suddenly, things don't seem as simple as whether someone is churched or unchurched.

Christian or not.

In or out.

The very language our culture uses has shifted to accommodate this new landscape. There are new disclaimers and perceptions when it comes to matters of the soul: Those who self-describe as "spiritual, but not religious"—individuals who like to associate with what they perceive as the positive elements of spirituality but not the negative associations of organized religion. Or consider the rise of the "nones"—the much-discussed adults who are religiously unaffiliated and who don't want to use any conventional label for their religious faith. And everywhere you turn, the prefix "post-" is being attached to matters of faith. Post-Christian. Post-denominational. Post-evangelical. Post-religious.

All these words and phrases describe a culture that is edging away from conventional Christianity as though secularization is the new normal. The culture seems to be saying, "Christianity? Been there, done that. Church? What's the point?"

Of course, that's not the whole story; Christianity remains vital to millions of people. Yet this disconnection from religion and church is a major part of what many people are feeling. The question this FRAME seeks to answer is set squarely against this cultural backdrop: In what ways does being part of a local faith community — a church — matter in this increasingly post-Christian setting?

As a pastor in New York City — one of the most post-Christian cities in America — Jon Tyson has been confronting these questions head-on for years. After taking a suburban "megachurch" model to the big city, Jon began to ask questions he hadn't before: How are our expectations for church being shaped by culture? What does a truly compelling church community look like? Can Christians — church wounds or not — still find life and purpose in the church? These questions shape the FRAME you're about to read, specifically focusing on how these questions are affecting younger generations.

When we focus on secularization among Millennials — the youngest generation of adults in America — we note some concerning trends. For a nation that has always prided itself on spiritual foundations, it becomes profoundly unsettling when nearly two-thirds of eighteen- to twenty-nine-year-olds with a Christian upbringing walk out of the church — perhaps never to return. Yet that is exactly what's happening, according to our research at Barna.

The national dialogue on the Millennial church exodus has caused many church leaders to ask some hard questions: How can we reach the young people we are losing? What can we do differently to engage those who have walked away with wounding experiences of church? And what does all this mean for the future of the church?

The Stats on Churchgoing

So if church is losing its influence, why bother? This is the question multitudes of hurting, disappointed, and disenchanted Americans — both young and old — are asking. Let's take a look at the underlying attitudes toward church in America today — and what this means for the future of the church.

In our research for this FRAME, we asked what, if anything, helps Americans grow in their faith. Respondents had a variety of answers — prayer, family or friends, reading the Bible, having children — but church did not make the top ten factors.

Though the church was once a cornerstone of American life, this is no longer the case. In fact, American adults today are divided somewhat evenly on the importance of attending church. While half (49%) say it is "somewhat" or "very" important, the other 51% say it is "not too" or "not at all" important. In fact, the nuances of the responses tell a story of opposites.

While the minority of the people we interviewed (40%) are neutral when it comes to attending church, many more had a firm opinion about the matter. What is shocking is that of the remaining 60%, people are essentially split: saying it is either "very" important (30%) or "not at all" important (30%).

Generationally, Millennials (those under 30) stand out as least likely to value church attendance — only two in ten believe it is important. The research shows more than a third of Millennials (35%) take an anti-church stance.

In contrast, Elders, or The Silent Generation, (those over 68) are the most likely (40%) to view church attendance as "very" important, compared to one-quarter (24%) who deem it "not at all" important. Boomers (ages 49–67) and Gen Xers (ages 30–48) fall in the middle of these polar opposites.

So in light of these shifting spiritual attitudes, who actually still goes to church?

While tens of millions of Americans attend church each weekend, the practice has declined in recent years. In fact, regular attenders used to be people who went to church three or more weekends each month. Now, a regular church attender is someone who shows up once a month.

Furthermore, the percentage of people who

What's made your
FAITH GROW?

When asked what, if anything, has helped your faith or spirituality grow, Millennials had a variety of answers. **But, church? It didn't even make the top 10.**

01/ *Prayer*

02/ *Family or friends*

03/ *Reading the Bible*

04/ *Having children*

05/ *Relationship with Jesus*

06/ *Death or illness of a loved one*

07/ *My own beliefs*

08/ *Marriage or significant other*

09/ *God provided during hard times*

10/ *I have not grown spiritually*

have *not* attended a church function at all in the past six months surged from just one-third to nearly two-fifths of all Americans in the last decade. The shift is even more apparent among younger Americans, as more than half of Millennials and Gen Xers state they have not been to church in the last six months.

Yet a decline in church attendance doesn't necessarily mean spiritual engagement isn't happening; it simply means it's not as often found within church walls.

This is evident in the top reason cited for dropping out of church: 40% of those who don't find church important say it's because "I find God elsewhere." Following closely behind, the second top reason people give for not going to church is because it's not relevant to them personally (35%).

Millennials who are opting out of church cite three factors with equal weight in their decision: 35% cite the church's irrelevance, hypocrisy, and the moral failures of its leaders as reasons to check out of church altogether. In addition, two out of ten unchurched Millennials say they feel God is missing in church, and one out of ten senses that legitimate doubt is prohibited, starting at the front door.

Perhaps more poignant than reasons not to turn up for church are the motivations of those who do—even against the grain of the overall population.

Among the minority of adults who believe church is very important, they cite two reasons for this above the rest: to be closer to God (44%) and to learn more about God (27%). Additionally, 22% say they go to church because the Bible teaches community with other believers.

For Millennials, the generation most at risk of rejecting church, the reasons for choosing church are telling. More than half (54%) say they go because they value closeness with God. Fewer than one in ten say they go because the Bible says to gather with believers (compared to 24% of other generations). And despite the perception of Millennials' civic-mindedness and desire to "make a difference," only one in ten Millennials say they go to church to be God's hands and feet in the world.

Denominational differences also appear in personal decisions to stay in church. After "to be closer to God," Catholics cite their top reasons for attending church as the fact that they always attended church (28%), the fact that the church is God's hands and feet in the world (20%) and the desire to be a part of a community (19%). Protestants' top reason is based in personal development more than tradition— 35% say they attend church to learn more about God. Closely following, 28% say their church involvement is a direct result of the Bible's teaching to live in and with a church body.

The Push and Pull of Church

Although people cite their primary reasons for attending church as growing closer to God and learning more about him, Barna Group finds such closeness is a rare occurrence. Fewer than two out of ten churchgoers feel close to God on even a monthly basis. Additionally, while almost two-thirds of those who value church attendance go to learn more about God, fewer than one in ten (6%) who have ever been to church say they learned something about God or Jesus the last time they attended. In fact, the majority of people (61%) say they did not gain any significant or new insights regarding faith when they last attended.

Of course, it's easy to fling accusations against "the church" as a faceless, disembodied, power-that-be. But what is bringing—or driving away—Americans to the church on a local level?

By far, preaching and teaching are the most consequential considerations for choosing a local church. Among those who find attending church important, nearly 40% cite this as the main reason for choosing to call their current church home. Next to the sermon, worship style is a common deciding factor—27% say this has influenced their decision in finding a local church. Worship style is especially a strong influencer among Protestants (40%), while for Catholics, family tradition is a primary factor in local church attendance—38% say their upbringing, or their spouse's upbringing, in a church is a personal draw. And the real estate maxim "location, location, location" bears strongly on church choice for two demographics: Catholics (29%) and Millennials (21%).

The data shows two trends, often at crosscurrents. Adults are aware of their very real spiritual needs, yet they are increasingly dissatisfied with the church's attempt to meet those spiritual needs and are turning elsewhere.

While America is nearly evenly split on the question, "Do we still need churches?" Christians need to be able to answer the follow-up question: "*Why* do we still need churches?"

For the spiritual-but-not-religious, the self-identified post-religious, for those hurt by the church, and for those who experience God more fully outside of the church building, this remains an aching question. And how the Christian community answers it will determine its own future. ◆

SACRED ROOTS

Why the Church Still Matters

THE FRAME

BY JON TYSON

"I'm not sure I believe in the church."

"I don't even know what the church *is*."

"I've been going my whole life, and I just don't see the point anymore."

I'm a pastor. In New York City. To people primarily under the age of fifty. So these aren't uncommon words for me to hear. I hear them all the time from people on the street—people who, for whatever reason, decided to come to our church that morning for the first time in ten years. I hear them from neighbors and baristas and the guy sitting next to me on the subway.

But I wasn't hearing them that day from a stranger who happened to ask me what I do for a living. I wasn't hearing them from a childhood-Episcopalian-turned-atheist who had a bone to pick.

No, these words were coming from my wife.

When I was twenty-eight years old, I left a great-paying ministry in a suburban Central Florida megachurch to start a new church in New York City with some friends. Church planting wasn't as popular then as it is now, and it felt like this was the most important thing in the world. It felt like we were going to do something that mattered. Something profound. Something important and substantial in our generation. Maybe even something biblical in its proportions. We wanted to show the world Christianity was still a thing of beauty; that grace and redemption and community and hope could still win out at the end of the day in a broken world. And we wanted to see if this preposterous thing called church could actually work in one of the most post-religious cities in America[1] — a worldwide cultural hub known for its great need amid its great sophistication.

So we sold our homes, most of our possessions, paid off each other's debts like we'd read in the book of Acts, and headed out for New York City. We were a group of friends who loved each other, and we couldn't believe the dream in our hearts was slowly becoming the story of our lives.

The culture shock was profound and immediate. New Yorkers were aggressive, busy, and didn't seem to have much time for talking or listening. The trains were confusing, the cost of living extraordinary, and our apartment, tiny. The pace of life was insane, and we wondered what we had gotten ourselves into.

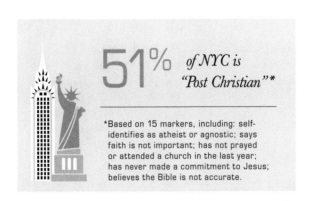

51% *of NYC is "Post Christian"**

*Based on 15 markers, including: self-identifies as atheist or agnostic; says faith is not important; has not prayed or attended a church in the last year; has never made a commitment to Jesus; believes the Bible is not accurate.

Even so, those early months were sublime. We felt as much wonder and adventure as we'd ever experienced. We didn't have much of a clue how to be a New York City church, so we ate and prayed and worshiped and celebrated, and slowly others began to join us. It was an amazing thing to see people who didn't know Jesus begin to grasp his message of grace and to watch their objections and hesitations bend under the weight of his love.

It felt like we were onto something — and *into* something that was bigger than mere human hands could hold.

We quickly outgrew our apartment as a meeting space. And about the time we began to outgrow the back room of a bar where we'd been gathering, we wondered if it was time to officially launch the church. So we booked a small theater in the Upper West Side of Manhattan, built a website, printed propaganda, bought equipment, and rehearsed the band. We formed teams and fasted and prayed. And then the big day came. That morning will stand out to me for the rest of my life. Over three hundred people packed themselves into the dark and musty space. Our seeds of faith had sprouted in the secular soil of New York, and we experienced our own version of Pentecost.

They came back the next Sunday. And they brought their friends, and we brought our friends, and our church was officially born. And then it grew — and it kept growing.

We were experiencing success — and yet I felt something

start to shift. A subtle emotional strain filled our lives. The slow-spreading hue of stress began to color everything we did. And we were doing a lot—programs and kids' care and small groups and all the stuff we knew had worked before. We launched outreach projects, pastoral care, justice ventures, and team trainings. Yet the more we seemed to do, the less we could truly give. The process was so slow you would not have been able to observe it at any given moment, but the end result was there: the joy was gone. It wasn't any one thing in particular but everything combined that led us to replace wonder with work, people with programs, organization with power, and dreams with duties.

And there were deeper problems than we could have imagined in our fledgling team. The stress of running a church was putting pressure on some deep cracks in our character. And as the cracks came to the surface, they began to break open for all to see.

One of our pastors had been sleeping with women he'd met on the Internet. He eventually abandoned his family. Several of our team members got into conflicts with one another that were as visceral as anything I had ever encountered. Our volunteers were exhausted and burning out, our finances were strained, our credit cards were maxed, and people's expectations were achingly unmet.

Yet despite all that, our church continued to grow. We didn't just add services and small groups, but locations. We were not just going to share the gospel, we thought, we were going to scale a movement. And by all outward appearances, we were.

Around this time I started to pick up on words that were beginning to dominate conversations—words like *options, convenience, church shopping, excellence,* being "better" than other churches, and the need to "compete." On one occasion, between services, I met with someone who had been attending our church for a while. This gentleman told me he had been visiting several churches, in fact, and while he liked different components of all of them, he wanted me to make the case for my church—why should he stop visiting the others and commit to ours?

His question took me aback. And I started to look around at the people joining our church. I realized they were almost all Christians from other churches. They had come because we were the new flavor of the month.

And I realized something else too: the unchurched people had all but stopped coming. When we were smaller and focused on relationships, non-Christians had been both fascinated and compelled by the love and practical servanthood they encountered. But it seemed the more we were known for how we did church—our style of church—the less non-Christians in our city seemed to care.

And then the problem became personal. About a week later, my wife, Christy, spoke those impossible words:

"I'm not sure I believe in the church. I don't even know what the church *is*. I've been going my whole life, and I just don't see the point anymore."

Her words stunned me into silence. I'd never heard my

wife talk like that before. I asked her what she meant. After all, hadn't we *moved here* for this church? And wasn't it going so well?

"We may look successful to the outside," she said. "But if we keep doing what we are doing, we will know in our hearts we just happen to be the cool church of the moment, built on buzz and vision talks, but not deep transformation or discipleship. And worse than that, we may fail in our mission. We may be entertaining Christians, but not helping those far from God make their way back to him."

Christy still loved Jesus, still loved people, and still believed the gospel was good news. She just wasn't sure the church we had created was producing the kind of disciples Jesus had in mind. Sure, we had become successful in the Christian subculture, but meanwhile, we were becoming irrelevant to the rest of the world.

From There to Here

I spent a few hours walking the streets of the city that night. In my heart, I knew she was speaking the truth, but it was hard to admit it to myself.

Here was my wife—on the inside of church—saying what I'd heard so many outsiders say. And I had a feeling her growing disillusionment with our church was deeply connected with the disillusionment I'd experienced from the guy on the subway, the bartender and the barista and the childhood-Episcopalian-turned-

59% *of Millennials who grew up in the church have dropped out at some point*

atheist. Their questions amounted to the same ringing indictment: What's the point of church, *really*?

Perhaps you've asked that very question yourself— because this isn't just a New York City problem. In fact, nearly one in six twentysomething Christians (59%) who grew up in the church say they had or have dropped out of going regularly.[2] Which means, if you're in your twenties and you grew up going to church, chances are you're one of the dropouts. Maybe you've come back, and maybe you haven't.

Maybe you left because you hated the hypocrisy. Maybe you were bored with the sermons. Maybe you no longer felt any of it was relevant to real life—to your life as it's being lived out right now. Maybe you started listening to your teachings on a podcast, found God in nature, or experienced a more authentic community at the local pub. Whatever the reason, at some point you no longer felt church was worth it.

In a recent magazine article in the *Atlantic*, one young

atheist who abandoned the church offers this reason for his disbelief: "Christianity is something that if you *really* believed it, it would change your life and you would want to change the lives of others. I haven't seen too much of that."[3] And that's it right there. If church isn't changing your life, then it's true, there really is no point.

But I believe it can change your life. I've *seen* it. And such a church *is* worth it. But creating that church will take some changes—from all of us. This can't just be about leaders shifting their strategies so more young people will like church again. Building a truly transformative and compelling church will take everyone—those of us leading, those of us showing up, those of us shopping, those of us who dropped out and remain skeptical on the fringes.

Our church is no longer the same church it was the day my wife said those startling words. We've undergone some major changes and many of them have been painful. But they've also been worth it. And, for us, those changes started at, well, the start ...

The Rise of the Early Church and the Decline of Ours

The growth of the early church is arguably the most remarkable sociological movement in history. The numbers are staggering. In AD 40 there were roughly one thousand Christians in the Roman Empire, but by AD 350 almost 30 million.[4] A remarkable 53% of the population had converted to the Christian faith.[5]

Sociologist Rodney Stark has spent much of his career
researching how this explosive growth happened. In *The
Triumph of Christianity*, he writes of Jesus:

> He was a teacher and miracle worker who spent
> nearly all of his brief ministry in the tiny and obscure
> province of Galilee, often preaching to outdoor
> gatherings. A few listeners took up his invitation to
> follow him, and a dozen or so became his devoted
> disciples, but when he was executed by the Romans
> his followers probably numbered no more than several
> hundred. How was it possible for this obscure Jewish
> sect to become the largest religion in the world?[6]

When you see who Jesus chose to found the church,
it seems even more implausible. The disciples were
untrained men who failed as often as they thrived. Peter
kept returning to fishing. James and John wanted to
call down fire on the very people Jesus came to save.
Thomas doubted, and Judas betrayed. They were selfish,
contentious, and they abandoned Jesus at his moment
of greatest need. Yet from these humble roots, baptized
in the power of Pentecost, the early church grew to
become not only the largest but the most influential
community in the Roman Empire.

All of this raises significant questions: What on earth
could have compelled half an empire to convert? How
could a Jewish political rebel, crucified on a Roman
cross, become the Savior of the empire that killed him?

The early church leaders didn't have the things we
now consider essential for our faith. They didn't have

official church buildings, vision statements, or core values. They had no social media, radio broadcasts, or celebrity pastors. They didn't even have the completed New Testament. Christ-followers were often deeply misunderstood, persecuted, and some gave their lives for their faith. Yet they loved and they served and they prayed and they blessed, and slowly, over hundreds of years, they brought the empire to its knees. They did it through love.

Getting to the Heart of the Church

In contrast to the early church, we live in one of the most well-resourced Christian cultures in history. Think about the ease, access, and cultural privilege with which we American Christians find ourselves today. We can get any number of Bible translations at a Walmart or Dollar Store. Podcasts are readily available from the most gifted and popular Bible teachers. We can watch video sermons, listen to live worship albums, and read in-depth studies in Greek and Hebrew. Many of us have entire collections of Bible software on our phones. We have Bible conferences, church growth conferences, denominational conferences, leadership conferences, missional conferences, church planting conferences, and even conferences for pastors and people who don't like church. We have Christian TV, Christian radio, short-term mission trips, and presidents who are interviewed about their personal relationships with Jesus Christ. And yet the church's influence, attendance, and ability to capture the imagination of the world seem mediocre at best. In his book *Roaring Lambs*, Bob Briner famously said:

> Do you honestly believe that our big churches and highly visible Christian leaders have brought about a movement that is taken seriously in this country? We feel we are making a difference because we are so important to ourselves. We have created a phenomenal subculture with our own media, entertainment, educational system and political hierarchy so that we have the sense that we're doing a lot. But what we've really done is create a ghetto that is easily dismissed by the rest of society.[7]

How could the early church capture the imagination of the empire, while we, with all our resources and rigor, are slowly losing influence in our culture?

I believe two major factors have negatively shaped people's expectations of what it means to be the church in our time: the entertaining church and the individualistic church.

Church as Entertainment

The impact of consumerism on American culture has been repeatedly discussed. From documentaries, the rise of Occupy Wall Street, and our media exposure on how the rest of the world lives, we understand the concept of consumerism and wonder about its implications for our culture. But we rarely ask how it forms our longings and expectations as disciples of Jesus. When we apply these same consumer standards to church, we end up approaching our Sunday worship with an attitude that can be summed up in this one simple phrase: "I want experts to put on exciting events that meet my expectations."

What in our nation hasn't been converted to a form of consumable entertainment? From housewives to handymen, pregnancy to porn, blockbusters to blogs, our media are constantly training us to expect things to be "amazing." It's not enough for things to be good or true or faithful. They have to earn and keep our attention. This has the double effect of making us increasingly passive in real life, while at the same time making us increasingly critical about the life we experience.

This leaks into what happens at church. We expect brilliance from the pulpit, but often accept mediocrity in our souls. What is presented up front is often exceptional, yet most of us live average lives. This can lead us to strive after incredible encounters while failing to pay attention to what God is actually doing around us. As Catholic theologian Vincent Miller says,

> Along with sporting events, rock concerts, shopping malls, and magazines, television provides images of the good life that bring virtual vicarious fulfillment. In the face of a spectacular world with which our everyday lives could never compete, we are reduced to passive spectators, consumers of illusions.[8]

If it's not "incredible" or "awesome," we begin to wonder if it's even worth our time. I have never heard a church leader say, "This is going to be pretty average, not very exciting, and probably hard, but it will form your character so you should deny yourself and come along for your own good and the good of others." No, everything is framed as an event not to be missed: "Our next series is going to be *amazing*, our small groups are going to be *incredible*, our new website is *unbelievable*, our kids' ministry is *fantastic*, and our pastor is *hilarious*."

But the hyped expectations don't match the depth of the issues many of us are wrestling with—things like abuse, abandonment, unemployment, divorce, bankruptcy, dead-end jobs, and heartbreaking relationships. Our lives are filled with the failed promises of consumer culture. What an indictment if the church proves to simply be another failed promise. The church should be the place we are not just promised more, but the place we can be vulnerable. It should be the place where, together, we can explore the mess and the grief and the joy and the sorrow.

In a "church as entertainment" culture, instead of seeking to be equipped as disciples of Jesus, we are slowly formed into consumers and critics who give ratings and reviews on a local church's performance. Our expectations of church have been shaped by what we expect from the rest of our lives. When someone hears about or first visits a church, the culture has already told them what matters. Rarely does a person enter a church thinking, "How can I honor these people as better than myself?" or "I wonder what ministries are struggling so I can use my gifts to help build up others?" Instead, most people come in with a subconscious rating and review system. We evaluate, grade, and critique every aspect of the service—from how convenient the parking and location are, how good the preaching is, how friendly the people are during the greeting time, how good the worship makes us feel, to how much we connected with the programs.

In our own FRAMES research, the majority of churchgoers admitted they chose their church either because they enjoyed the preaching (39%) or the worship style (27%). A few said it was because of the friendly people (18%). And among the top reasons for leaving a church? The sermons aren't good enough (25%) and the location is inconvenient (13%).

What's So Great About Your Church?

For those currently attending a church, these are the top three reasons they picked (and stuck with) that church:

39%
"I enjoy the preaching or teaching"

38%
"I agree with the teachings of that church"

27%
"I like the worship style"

27%
"My spouse or I was raised in that denomination"

18%
"It's friendly and welcoming"

What Would Make You Leave Your Church?

What makes for a good reason to leave your church? The following were strong enough reasons for most current church attenders:

63%
"Disagree with teachings or beliefs"

25%
"Disagree with a leadership decision"

16%
"Sermons aren't good enough"

13%
"In an inconvenient location"

11%
"Not involved enough in the community"

But when we expect the church to entertain us, it limits the church's ability to challenge us. Entertainment rarely transforms. Think about the last time you went to a concert. What did you experience? Perhaps incredible visuals, swelling emotions, a sense of community among fans, and the power of a group of people with the same style, taste, and aesthetic values. It can be very moving. But normally, after a concert, the number one question people ask is, "Where are we going to eat?" You don't normally leave these sorts of events reevaluating the kind of person you are becoming; you simply enjoy it and move on to the next thing.

Something similar happens when entertainment shapes the church. Our emotions may soar, we may have a shared sense of "us," and we may resonate with the experience, but rarely does entertainment sanctify our hearts. It rarely challenges the practices that form our character or shape our lives. It's hard to live the Sermon on the Mount with the whole of your life when your understanding of church is that it is like an exciting concert. The result may be that we overlook the things that make up our actual lives, the normal stuff that shapes who we become over the long haul. And it can cause us to miss our call. We don't exist for ourselves, but to embody the good news of Jesus to those around us.

Church for the Individual

The second defining force that has shaped many of today's Christians' view of church is radical individualism. This kind of individualism can be succinctly defined as "the sovereignty of self": self over others, self over community, self over inconvenience, and self over commitment. Our life and longings are formed around a vision of personal fulfillment at all costs. Everyone and everything exists for us. We want our lives to be an epic story in which we play the starring role. Yet when we consciously or subconsciously believe this, Jesus' words and Jesus' invitation can become tools we use to meet our own needs.

Consider the top two reasons practicing Christians told us they attend church: to be closer to God (43%) and to learn more about God (32%). While neither of those are bad reasons, they are self-focused reasons. The top two reasons people don't attend church are even more

Why do you
ATTEND CHURCH?

If you think it's important to attend church, chances are the
main reason you go is "to be closer to God." No matter their age,
denomination, or background, the majority of people who
value church cite this as their top reason for going to church.
After that, though, people's motivations tend to vary.

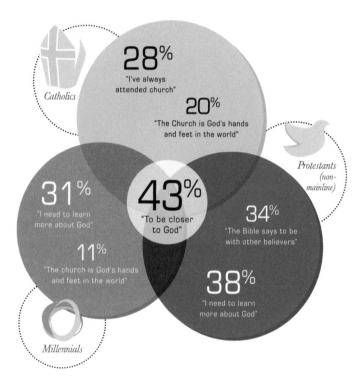

Catholics

28%
"I've always
attended church"

20%
"The Church is God's hands
and feet in the world"

*Protestants
(non-mainline)*

31%
"I need to learn
more about God"

43%
"To be closer
to God"

34%
"The Bible says to be
with other believers"

11%
"The church is God's hands
and feet in the world"

38%
"I need to learn
more about God"

Millennials

revealing: I find God elsewhere (40%) and church is not relevant to me personally (35%).

A few years ago, I began to see this more and more in the way people processed Jesus' call to discipleship. His call was scandalous. It was a call to die, to take up our cross; a call to self-denial. And it was a call to community, to put others' needs before our own desires, and to steward personal resources as a source of blessing and hope for the world. It wasn't a call to *find* ourselves, but to *lose* ourselves in him and to learn to lay down our lives for our brothers and sisters.

In fact, most of Jesus' invitations were not simply personal invitations to personal salvation; they were invitations to *communal* salvation—and shared responsibility as a result. Jesus made this clear when he said in John 13:34–35:

> "A new command I give you: Love one another. As I have loved you, so you must love one another. By this everyone will know that you are my disciples, if you love one another."

When radical individualism overshadows our faith, we will only process Jesus' teachings and wrestle with Jesus' call to discipleship as individuals. But according to Jesus himself, such individualistic treatment misses the full experience of faith.

Here are some common individualistic lenses through which we approach faith.

1 **The Public Level.** The first sphere is where we interact with the world—our career, hobbies, and

vocation. When it comes to the public sphere of life, we ask Jesus questions like, What should I do for a job? What are my gifts? How can the church help me reach my potential? In essence, this is where we see the role of the church as a chaplain to inspire us with spiritual fuel for the rest of the week.

2 **The Private Level.** The second sphere is that of our private lives—our home, finances, and intimate relationships. When it comes to this area of life, we are often seeking answers to questions like, How can I deal with my loneliness? What do I do with my sexuality? How can I figure out how to get out of debt? I would categorize most of these concerns under life skills. In the private realm, we see the church as a place to give us life coaching so we can get ahead and remain "balanced."

3 **The Personal Level.** This is the sphere of the heart— intimate and secret and often filled with doubt. Here, we ask, Can I trust God? How can I hear from God? How can I make sense of the difficult passages in the Bible? This, of course, is the level many churches are most familiar with.

There is nothing wrong with asking these questions of Jesus. After all, these are human questions. But if we always put our needs first, we have positioned ourselves as the master and Jesus as the servant. This may seem like quite the accusation, yet we indict ourselves in the simple expressions, "I didn't like the worship," or "I didn't get anything out of that sermon."

If the public, private, and personal are the only or

defining levels through which we respond to Jesus' call, we have missed something critical in his message. We have skipped over the call to follow Jesus in a larger body.

Project "Self" vs. the People of God

In his excellent book *Atonement for a Sinless Society*, Alan Mann argues that modern life can be summed up in the phrase "Project Self."[9] Project Self means we are sovereign over our own lives, and all of our energy, passion, learning, striving, imagination, and resources should be directed toward the end goal of fulfilling our personal dreams. It's easy to see how deeply this is embedded in our culture, but it's not as obvious that many people unconsciously use Jesus—and the local church—as a means to further the advancement of their Project Self.

Remember that young man in the *Atlantic* article? "Christianity is something that if you *really* believed it," he said, "it would change your life and you would want to change the lives of others. I haven't seen too much of that."

That cuts to the heart of it. A faith that has been co-opted by entertainment and individualism has lost its compelling force. Maybe the world is bored with the church because they expect to see something different, but they see only a reflection of themselves. Jesus said when the salt loses its saltiness, it is good for nothing but to be trampled underfoot (see Matthew

Why don't you
ATTEND CHURCH?

Across age and denomination, the top two reasons unchurched Americans said they didn't think attending church was important were always the same:

40%

"I find God elsewhere"

35%

"Church is not relevant to me personally"

5:13). And maybe that is what's happening. Because we have failed to become a clear, compelling counterculture, the world looks at what the church has become, shrugs, and says, "I can do without the hypocrisy and guilt. I think I'll figure life out on my own."

If we are honest, we will confess we know in our hearts our personal fulfillment comes from something other than entertaining events or individualist pursuits. We long for something deeper. Something below the surface of a public, private, and personal call. We long to put our roots into something deep, something profound, something mysterious and demanding, and something that calls us out of the small story of Project Self into the masterpiece of redemption in the kingdom of God.

We know we are not saved just to be individuals who are going to heaven when we die, but to be a part of a new community—those who put the love of Jesus on display for the world to see.

But what would something like that look like in a culture like ours?

Planting Sacred Roots in Secular Soil

So how do we move past this cultural stagnation? How do we press into a more compelling expression of church and get the roots of the gospel into the soil of this new kind of community? I think it begins by getting below the surface of a consumer culture and responding to the call of Jesus in a different way.

I mentioned earlier that our society has conditioned us to respond to Jesus at three common levels.

Public—"What do I do with my career?"

Private—"What do I do with my social life?"

Personal—"What do I do in my heart?"

But I believe that below these popular responses, there is a profoundly deeper one—a call our hearts long to hear.

If an entertainment-driven, individualistic view of church is defined as "experts putting on exciting events to meet personal expectations," then the primal call of

Jesus reminds us the church is more daring, subversive, transformative, and provocative than we have been numbed to believe — that we are not destined to be passive spectators but active agents of grace and redemption in the middle of the brokenness of our world.

In other words, there is a fourth level:

> **Primal** — "Denying myself for the sake of communal discipleship and mission."

This kind of transformation, of course, will take good, hard work. I believe recovering the church's purpose in all its beauty will require four conscious, communal shifts. Together these shifts have the power to transform our churches from consumer centers in the Christian ghetto to provocative countercultures for the common good and renewal of our world. So what are these shifts?

1. From Dabbling to Devotion

> "All the believers were one in heart and mind" (Acts 4:32).

Most of our discipleship, we'll admit if we're honest, looks like it's taking place on the wrong side of the cross. Personal ambition, rivalry, and selfishness often described the disciples before Christ's death and resurrection. But they were deeply transformed when the Spirit came at Pentecost. Listen to the description in Acts 2:42 – 47 of the previously fickle followers of Jesus after they were baptized in the Spirit (emphasis added):

> They *devoted* themselves to the apostles' teaching and

to fellowship, to the breaking of bread and to prayer. Everyone was filled with awe at the many wonders and signs performed by the apostles. All the believers were together and had everything in common. They sold property and possessions to give to anyone who had need. Every day they continued to meet together in the temple courts. They broke bread in their homes and ate together with glad and sincere hearts, praising God and enjoying the favor of all the people. And the Lord added to their number daily those who were being saved.

We too are called to live on the Spirit-empowered side of the cross, where we turn away from the confines of building up our own kingdoms to a self-denying, countercultural community of discipleship and mission.

The word *devotion* modifies everything else we see in the text. The intensity and intentionality of the lives of the early church members set them apart from much of the religious activity of their day. Faith was not an addition to life, but a reframing of life itself.

In his excellent book *Multiplying Missional Leaders*, Mike Breen has beautifully described the nature of devotion in terms of how we steward the capital — the resources or wealth — of our lives. And how we spend our capital is how we spend our lives. Breen identifies several areas of capital: spiritual, physical, financial, intellectual, and relational.[10]

When we let the world shape our vision and desire, we commonly end up spending those resources in the following order of priority:

1 Financial
2 Physical
3 Intellectual
4 Relational
5 Spiritual

We give our lives to get ahead financially. We work, spend, and accumulate debt, and then repeat the cycle again and again. We obsess over our bodies and how we present ourselves physically. We devote ourselves to our clothes, our appearance, and our health in almost religious ways. We get an education so we can put letters after our names. We study and debate and form opinions. We often fall into the trap of believing that just because we think something is true, we have done something about it. We can slam how the wealthy spend their money, yet we may or may not stop to realize our spending habits reflect the same sorts of patterns, just with smaller price tags attached. Then only after we have devoted ourselves to these pursuits, we give whatever leftovers we have to our families. And if there's anything left after that, we care for our souls.

Jesus describes this in the Sermon on the Mount as the things the pagans run after (see Matthew 6:32). Unfortunately, today the "pagans" and the Christians seem to be running after the same things. According to our research, a nearly equal number of churched people and unchurched people describe themselves as totally committed to getting ahead in life (54% vs. 59%), stressed out (33% vs. 38%), in serious financial debt (16% vs. 15%), concerned about the future (80% vs. 79%) and lonely (17% vs. 20%). But as Christians, we are called to seek first the kingdom of God.

Does church
MAKE A DIFFERENCE?

When it comes to the big stuff in life, do people who go to
church look, act, or feel any differently than those who don't?
For the most part, it would seem the answer is "no."

I would describe myself as...

"Totally committed to getting
ahead in life"

Unchurched	59%
Churched	54%

"Deeply spiritual"

	18%
	69%

"Stressed out"

	38%
	33%

"In serious financial debt"

	15%
	16%

"Dealing with addiction"

	5%
	6%

"Concerned about the future"

	79%
	80%

"Trying to find a few good
friends"

	38%
	39%

"Putting my career first"

	21%
	14%

"Lonely"

	20%
	17%

"Happy"

	79%
	86%

"Too busy"

	35%
	36%

"Fulfilling my calling in life"

	61%
	77%

We must reverse the order in which we spend our capital. A life of devotion would mean we spend and prioritize our lives in this countercultural way:

1 Spiritual
2 Relational
3 Physical
4 Intellectual
5 Financial

A primal church is called to devote itself to the radical pursuit of God, walking with him and delighting in his presence. We create time to steward emotional energy to bear one another's burdens. We use our strength and energy to serve one another in practical ways—cleaning, moving, celebrating, fixing, and working. We make sure we get enough rest so we can be fully present to what is happening in the lives of those around us. We eat and exercise to steward our bodies as holy temples where God's presence dwells. Although sharpening our intellect is important, it does not come to the detriment of or distraction from our love and lives. And last, we seek ways to steward what we have, practicing generosity, not letting the desire for more choke out the work God wants to do in our lives.

Spending our capital in this order is a tangible way of practicing devotion—of loving God with all our hearts, minds, souls, and strength, and loving our neighbors as ourselves. A church filled with people like this, who are not just living for themselves but *spending* themselves on behalf of one another, is a church with people who have emotional energy to listen without distraction, time to walk others through the mess of addiction or divorce, commitment to invest in teenagers trying to make sense out of faith and life, and margin to savor and celebrate the things that are often lost in the frenzy of modern life. A church like this is unlike anything our culture has truly seen.

It's not just a pipe dream—I've seen it here and there, and you've likely seen glimpses of it too. One family in our church community has passionately committed themselves to being disciples of Jesus in the context of the city. He works in finance, she is a teacher, and they have small children they care for amid the demands of their careers. This description could apply to a lot of families today, but one quality makes this family stand apart: they're always available. No matter what's on their plate, they're always offering to serve, give, and love.

I once pulled them aside and asked how they managed to do this when everyone else seemed so overwhelmed. His reply astounded me: "I told my boss what my priorities are, and how many hours a week I'm willing to work. I told him I was only going to give so much to my job so I could live out what is important to me in the other areas of my life." His boss told him he was committing career suicide and that he would never rise above middle management. "That is a price I am very willing to pay," my friend said.

Academic Noam Chomsky once famously said the vision of modern life is an individual alone in a room, looking at a screen.[11] We know we are created for more than this. Jesus longs for us to live remarkably different lives than the world around us by devoting ourselves to different things. God's heart is that we might shift from dabbling in church to devoting ourselves to his kingdom in such a way that the world is jarred out of its idolatry by the intensity of our communal passion. And in a world of passive distraction, passionate devotion gains attention. It can shake the imagination of the empire once again.

2. From Transience to Permanence

> "As I urged you when I went into Macedonia, stay there in Ephesus" (1 Timothy 1:3).

The second shift the church needs to make is to take the reality of "place" seriously, to model the kingdom of God long enough so people get a tangible sense of what it truly is.

This is a massive shift for a nation of transient, rootless individuals — the average American moves every five years.[12] We are a people who drift across the continent following economic forces that not only impact our wallets but the relationships in our lives. In fact, it's safe to say the central metaphor that shapes our cultural consciousness is that of a journey. Always moving, always one foot out the door, always wondering what is over the horizon in the next town, job, relationship, or season.

Transience has become second nature, which is perhaps why we don't give the effect of restlessness on our souls much thought. Even less do we consider how it affects the health of our local church.

In his book *Here is New York*, E. B. White describes several different kinds of people who interact with a city. There are natives and locals, and the young and ambitious, but there is a third category: the locusts.[13] These are the people who live outside of the city where life is easy but commute downtown to take advantage of its opportunity and resources. They don't pay taxes, they don't raise their families within the city limits, and they don't wrestle with the city's challenges. They come, they take, and they leave.

This is how many of us live today. We move into a new area, buy a house in a neighborhood we like, put the kids in school, and get on with our lives. We "shop" for a church but rarely deeply commit because we always want to keep our options open or be ready for the next move. It's difficult to fully commit anywhere (or to anyone) because we never expect to stay. We come, we take, and we leave. To deal with this lack of commitment, churches used to have the practice of transferring membership. When someone moved to a new place, the last community would vouch for their character and faith. It was an attempt to weave the threads of faith into the fabric of mobile lives. But even that sort of continuity is dissolving. Having pastored thousands of people in the last ten years, I have never once had someone ask to transfer their membership to our church.

Yet the reality is that relationships take time to form. To love our neighbor means we have to know our neighbor. Beatrix Tafoya, one of our leaders at Trinity Grace Church, often says, "In other times of history the great commission was to go, but maybe the great commission in our generation is to stay." For those of us called to serve God in a Western context, these are words worth considering.

One of the definitive ways the early church shook the world was with their response and commitment to the places they lived. Cities in the Roman Empire were often places of crime, disease, and death. Fires would break out and destroy communities, but the real fear was of plagues. When a plague hit a city, it could devastate up to half of the population.

10 **LEAST** CHURCHED CITIES
in America

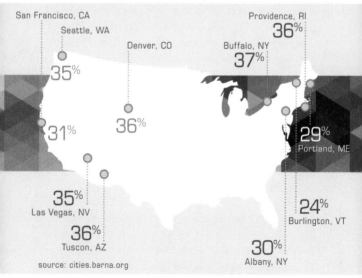

San Francisco, CA

Seattle, WA
35%

Denver, CO
36%

31%

35%
Las Vegas, NV

36%
Tuscon, AZ

Providence, RI
36%

Buffalo, NY
37%

29%
Portland, ME

24%
Burlington, VT

30%
Albany, NY

source: cities.barna.org

*Percentages represent the churchgoing population in each city

Dionysius, writing sometime around AD 260 at the height of a great epidemic, wrote:

> Most of our brother Christians showed unbounded love and loyalty ... heedless of danger, they took charge of the sick, attending to their every need and ministering to them in Christ, and with them departed this life serenely happy; for they were infected by others with the disease, drawing on themselves the sickness of their neighbors and cheerfully accepting their pains. Many, in nursing and curing others, transferred their death to themselves and died in their stead.

Does this sound like the church you know? He goes on to say,

> The heathen behaved in the very opposite way. At the first onset of the disease, they pushed the sufferers away and fled from their dearest, throwing them into the roads before they were dead and treated unburied corpses as dirt, hoping thereby to avert the spread and contagion of the fatal disease; but do what they might, they found it difficult to escape.[14]

Imagine that a deadly virus broke out in the place you live. Most people would probably flee as far away as they could. But the early church took Jesus' call seriously. Believing they had eternal life and that Jesus' command to lay down our lives for one another was to be taken literally, they stayed to care for those around them. This had a profound effect on the world. Roman historian Eusebius, a church leader of the time, describes the way these acts of love impacted their generation: "[The Christians'] deeds were on everyone's lips, and they glorified the God of the Christians. Such actions convinced them that they alone were pious and truly reverent to God."[15]

To move toward rootedness in our discipleship at Trinity Grace Church, we have reclaimed the idea of the "parish." We define a parish as a geographic area of spiritual responsibility. We are not called to just care for church members, but whole communities—modeling the sacrificial love of Jesus in a particular context. This means that what happens in my parish is my responsibility.

Many in our church community have started to take this call seriously. They have stepped into problem areas in the community, acting as chaplains and police liaisons. They've forged relationships with local business owners, joined the PTA, launched community associations, opened arts programs, and led initiatives to restore public parks. And they have done all this in Jesus' name, with humility and love, as servants of the community. As a result, we have seen the beginning of a shift. We have seen cynics' hearts soften, atheists begin to doubt their doubt, and lonely people find a home in a community where they experience healing and acceptance. And one life at a time, Jesus is becoming a topic of conversation in the places where we live.

This, I think, is the kind of church the world truly wants—a church that sees God's activity as relevant to all of life, not just Sunday morning events. Sometimes all a church is known for in a community is causing traffic problems or owning prime pieces of land they don't pay property tax on. We want our communities to be thrilled Christians live in the neighborhood. We want the kingdom of God to come into our neighborhoods as it is in heaven. Committing to live and love in a place for the long haul is a powerful step in this direction.

The only way the church will learn to thrive and bear fruit in a given context is if we commit to planting sacred roots in secular soil — deep roots.

3. From Preference to Proximity

"Follow God's example, therefore, as dearly loved children and walk in the way of love, just as Christ loved us and gave himself up for us as a fragrant offering and sacrifice to God" (Ephesians 5:1 – 2).

The third shift required to capture the imagination of the world is that of proximity, which often determines our capacity to love people well. Put simply, it's hard to love people the way Jesus calls us to if we never see them.

In the book *The Intentional Christian Community Handbook*, the author writes,

The twentieth century will be remembered as an age of wondrous creativity, when Americans voluntarily shattered their lives into distant and dissonant fragments. America's industries learned how to assemble atomic bombs, airplanes, iPads and the genetic codes of life itself in the same era that American society disassembled the ancient overlap of family, food, faith and the field of work. Americans reached for the stars as they withered their roots, inhabited space but lost any sense of place.[16]

The way our modern lives are organized makes it incredibly challenging to be the kind of church Jesus had in mind, even if we want to with all our hearts. It's hard to demonstrate sacrificial love for others when we only see them every other week in a programmed Christian event. If we're going to love like we're called, it will require far more intentionality than bumping into each other at the coffee bar after the service or shaking hands across the aisle during the morning greeting or passing of the peace.

I live in a part of the city with a large community of Orthodox Jews. Every Friday night the streets are lined with people walking to the synagogue for Shabbat, and grocery stores are careful to highlight their kosher options. Because of their observance of the Sabbath, Jews often live within walking distance of the synagogue, and because they choose to work only six days a week in our crazy 24/7 world, they are intentional about the kinds of jobs they take and the industries they enter. They do this so they can see each other, raise their children together, share a common faith and life, and thrive as people in a given context for the long haul. They are a people choosing to live in close proximity with each other so their collective vision can come to life.

Contrast this with how many of us choose where we

10 MOST CHURCHED CITIES
in America

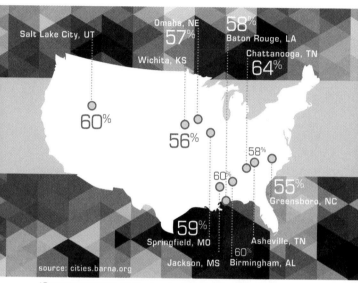

Salt Lake City, UT

Omaha, NE
57%

58%
Baton Rouge, LA

Wichita, KS

Chattanooga, TN
64%

60%

56%

58%

60%

55%
Greensboro, NC

59%
Springfield, MO

Asheville, TN

Jackson, MS

60%
Birmingham, AL

source: cities.barna.org

*Percentages represent the churchgoing population in each city

live today—we make our choices based on safety, school quality, or the number of nearby amenities. Now, there is nothing inherently wrong with this, but there is no kingdom intentionality in it either. Jesus calls us to arrange our lives in such a way that we remove the obstacles and pattern our habits so we can be tangibly present in each other's stories.

First Thessalonians 2:8 puts it like this: "Because we loved you so much, we were delighted to share with you not only the gospel of God but our lives as well."

Though our culture values autonomy and treats privacy as a fundamental human right, the hunger for true community remains. After all, nearly one in five adults admits to being lonely (whether or not they're in church). Our broken families have not killed our desire for family, but reconfigured it. We seek belonging and acceptance from urban tribes that flow in and out of our lives. Think about the rise of TV shows like HBO's *Girls* and *Entourage*, and the shows *Community* and *Modern Family*—all narratives of ordinary people searching for a place to belong. We long for a place where we can be known and loved, challenged and encouraged. And yet many of us don't consider that the church could be such a place. When we asked practicing Christians why they chose their current church, more than three times as many listed the quality of the preaching (46%) over the quality of relationships (14%). And when asked why they think it's important to attend church, only one in ten listed being part of a community as one of those reasons. But Jesus did not say Christians would be known for the quality of their sermons. He said they would be known by the quality of their love for each other.

What would the church look like if the members chose to buy homes in the same neighborhoods or subdivisions, lived in the same apartment buildings or blocks, and sent their children to the same schools? What would love look like if it showed up dozens of times a week in small but profound ways: meals cooked, prayers prayed, songs sung, Scripture studied, games played, parties thrown, tears shed, reconciliation practiced, resources given? What if we stopped attending community groups and became groups of communities? What if our homes stopped being the places we hid from the world but havens to which the world comes for healing?

Christians are not just called to share a worldview or a theological commitment, but hearts and lives, consolations and desolations, and the big moments and small moments that form who we are. We need people in close proximity who see us when we are not performing, when our guard is down and our hearts are laid bare. We need our character to be observed and our habits known.

Of course, practicing this sort of community will require real discernment. We will have to wrestle with situations that touch every detail of our lives. Should we move to another state to pursue a job? Should we put elderly parents in assisted living or invite them to live with us if they want? Should we move to a different neighborhood if the schools are bad? At this time in history, I believe the church is called to *wrestle deeply* with these issues. One way to do this is to process our life choices through a communal lens, one that takes into consideration the effect of our choices — not just on our families but on our church and community. I think this process, as well as the outcome, shows the world a different way to live.

I can't help but imagine how beautiful and powerful the church would be if we were not known for "where we went to church," but how we *are* the church, if we did not judge church by the excellence of its programs but by the excellence of our lives. As early Christian author Tertullian said in his *Apology*, "It is our care of the helpless, our practice of loving kindness that brands us in the eyes of many of our opponents. 'Only look,' they say, 'look how they love one another!' "[17]

4. From Belief to Practices

"Do not merely listen to the word, and so deceive yourselves. Do what it says" (James 1:22).

The final shift the church should make is to reorient faith from something we believe in to a lifestyle defined by distinctly Christian practices. This may seem obvious, but it's not easy.

We may live in one of the most spiritually deceptive times in the history of the church. We are so overwhelmed with Christian content that it is not humanly possible to put into practice even half of what we hear. Couple this with a classroom approach to discipleship, and our faith is often reduced to the transfer of information from one head to another.

But in Acts 2:42–47, we see how the believers at Pentecost translated the outpouring of the Spirit's power into tangible living. I have highlighted important practices in italics:

They devoted themselves to the apostles' teaching and to *fellowship*, to the *breaking of bread* and to *prayer*. Everyone was filled with awe at the many wonders and signs performed by the apostles. All the believers were together and had *everything in common. They sold* property and possessions *to give* to anyone who had need. Every day *they continued to meet* together in the temple courts. *They broke bread* in their homes and *ate together* with glad and sincere hearts, *praising God* and enjoying the favor of all the people. And the Lord added to their number daily those who were being saved.

It would be unthinkable to read, "They were filled with the Holy Spirit, and he corrected their theology, and then they went on living, for the most part, ordinary lives." We are called to be disciples of Jesus, not just believers. We are called to do what Jesus taught, to practice his ways, to make his character and kingdom tangible, not just repeat what he said to others.

At the end of the day, how we live is what we really believe. Everything else is just talk.

When I was sixteen years old, I left high school to become an apprentice butcher. I signed a legal document indenturing myself to four years of training. My apprenticeship began with everything everyone else didn't want to do: cleaning scraps, scrubbing equipment, making sausages, and unloading trucks. I began to learn about the tools of the trade: the sharpness of a knife, the power of a saw, and the spices in the recipes for seasoned meats. I was given simple tasks under close direction. I wasn't allowed to move on to a new area of learning until I had internalized the previous skill, which sometimes took a matter of hours and sometimes months.

I also attended a technical college. I took classes on agriculture, management, hygiene, business, and supply chains. But for every couple of weeks in class, I spent six months working under the mentorship of practicing butchers. My exams were not simply written tests — the primary test was whether or not I could do the work of butchering. Over the course of time, lesson by lesson, mentor by mentor, and through the integration of knowledge, character, experience, and skill, I finally became a butcher.

My career has taken quite a turn since that apprenticeship. And yet I still benefit from those years of apprenticeship, which taught me the true importance of putting my skills and knowledge *to work*. After all, a person with a knowledge of meat who cannot actually prepare and serve it is not a butcher but a food critic.

When you look at the ministry of Jesus, you see him apprenticing his disciples, not just teaching them. To take on the way of Jesus wasn't simply to take on his worldview or interpretation of the Scriptures; it was to take on his lifestyle — to learn how to think, love, act, relate, practice, embody, and model the kingdom of God. In the Sermon on the Mount, Jesus gave a clear picture of the practices he wanted his disciples to live out:

- Kindness over judgment

- Forgiveness over vengeance

- Purity and faithfulness in our sexuality

- Turning the other cheek

- Loving, praying for, and blessing our enemies

- Praying and fasting for God and not people

- Giving in secret

- Seeking God's kingdom and not material riches

- Seeking God radically through persistent prayer

- Building our life on observing these practices and obeying Jesus' words

We are called to love the outcast, challenge hypocrisy, lay down our lives for one another, celebrate the good and the true and the beautiful, and give generously— all while seeking God and finding him in mysterious and miraculous ways. And then, when the challenges and trials of life come, we will be deeply rooted in God's love, and his grace will enable us to walk with perseverance and joy.

Church can certainly be a place where Christians are informed by teaching, but God's heart is for the church to become a place that equips people for kingdom living.

I think about my friend Diana. She has lived in the city for years and is successful in one of New York's prominent fashion houses. But she has only come to church recently, and her life has changed by joining a community that lives out their faith. She has learned to hear God's voice through word and worship, and then implement what the Spirit prompts her to do in a secular, challenging environment. It's changed her attitude, demeanor, relationships, and even her work results. At a recent performance review, she was given glowing praise for her latest work and leadership. When asked what had happened to bring about so much change, Diane replied, "I've joined a church."

Putting Sacred Roots into Secular Soil

Jesus modeled all of these shifts in the most beautiful way: He prioritized his life around loving people. He didn't dabble with love but *devoted* himself to his disciples. He washed their feet and restored them after they failed. He died for their (and everyone's) sins, and then rose again on their behalf. He came to us to secure a *place* for us. He takes his kingdom and this earth seriously. He has been preparing a place for us, and one day the beautiful city will come to earth, and we will dwell with him forever.

Jesus also arranged his life so he was in intimate *proximity* to his disciples. He did daily life with them,

"ATTENDING CHURCH IS NOT IMPORTANT TO ME BECAUSE ..."

"It's not relevant to me personally"

35%	Millennials
37%	Gen-X
37%	Baby Boomers
21%	Elders

watching them, loving them, teaching them, and training them. And through his Spirit, he is not just with us, but in us, the hope of glory (see Colossians 1:27). He also put his love into *practice*—healing the sick, confronting hypocrisy, welcoming the outcast, embracing the leper, and ultimately giving his life in love. That is why when we respond to the call of Jesus to *deny ourselves for the sake of a communal discipleship and mission,* the church looks less like the world and more like Jesus. And a church that looks and loves like Jesus in the midst of our culture would be an almost irresistible thing.

On the day of Pentecost, Peter said that, because of the promise of the Father, the Spirit would be poured out on all flesh. He said, "Your young men will see visions, your old men will dream dreams" (Acts 2:17). Many younger people in our culture have no vision for the church, and they see it as increasingly irrelevant (the number one reason Millennials give for not attending church). Many older people have lost their dreams. The hardness of life and the distance of time have muted

"ATTENDING CHURCH IS NOT IMPORTANT TO ME BECAUSE ..."

"I find God elsewhere"

30%		Millennials
40%		Gen-X
42%		Baby Boomers
57%		Elders

their expectations of what God can do in their lives and through a body of believers (they told us they don't attend church because they find God elsewhere).

But when the Spirit is poured out on the people of God, something changes. Young people recover their vision. They begin to see the possibilities for the people of God. Older people recover the dream of their hearts and believe the best of their days could still be ahead. The church, in its very nature, is called to be a movement of dreamers and visionaries — a prophetic force salting the injustice and decay of our world and unleashing the presence of God.

A few weeks ago, my wife and I picked up our conversation about the nature and purpose of the church. But this time, I didn't walk away with a knot in my stomach. It was a conversation filled with joy and laughter as we reflected on the hopeful way Jesus is forming his people into this unique community here in New York. Rather than merely rating our services on a performance scale, people are taking the call of Jesus seriously. They are living lives of passionate devotion and sacrifice across the neighborhoods of the city, and they are committing to stay in the city, often at great cost. They have a vision of a kingdom that is bigger than the success of any individual life. They are moving closer to one another with intentionality so they can love each other deeply and weave their lives more closely in love. And they are not only hearing but practicing the teachings of Jesus — sharing resources, serving the poor, pursuing holiness, studying the Scriptures, coming together for prayer, and welcoming the stranger.

Slowly, but powerfully, the mustard seeds of the gospel are breaking through the secular soil of New York City into living plants where people are finding rest in the shade.

The Church as Preview

I was attending a movie with my son recently and, during several of the previews, Nathan leaned over to me and said, "We have *got* to see that." It got me thinking about the art of the movie trailer. There are so many films, and we have such little time, that those two-minute clips have to reach into our hearts and garner that coveted response, "I *have* to see that."

The church is like that—a compelling preview of what is to come, intended to draw the world in to see the full picture. Your life, as part of the church, is meant to be a preview as well. You are called to offer a picture of how beautiful self-denial, shared discipleship, and mission can be in a culture of shallow entertainment and radical individualism.

We live in a world that so often looks at the church and, seeing hypocrisy, exclusivity, and stringent rules, says, "I don't want any part in that."

So, together, as Christ's church, may we put the brilliance of Jesus on display in such a way that elicits only one response from a watching world: "I *have* to be part of that." ◆

SACRED ROOTS
Why the Church Still Matters

RE/FRAME

BY RICH VILLODAS

Growing up in one of the most dangerous neighbor-hoods in Brooklyn, the last thing I thought I'd be was a pastor.

But God surprised me. Today, at thirty-four years old, I find myself pastoring one of the most multi-ethnic churches in the US. As Søren Kierkegaard writes, "Life can only be understood backwards; but it must be lived forwards." As I look back on my journey, I understand more fully how I arrived where I am today.

I grew up in a Puerto Rican home that was indifferent toward Christianity. Though my parents had me baptized in the Catholic Church, our family members were all in a church together very few times.

All of that changed in the summer of 1999.

I had just arrived home from seeing my suddenly ex-girlfriend, who had dumped me after three years of our teenage relationship. I was broken, hurt, and in need of consolation. That night, my brother and three younger sisters were heading out to a small neighborhood church they'd been invited to. My parents weren't going, because for one thing my father was coming off a rough hangover from the night before. But I decided to go. As soon as I left the house, as my father told me later, he heard a voice say—"Follow him." To everyone's surprise, my parents showed up at the church fifteen minutes into the service—my father still in his pajamas.

That night, the speaker preached on Ezekiel 37, the story of the valley of dry bones. After the sermon, he invited people to make a decision to follow Christ. And I responded. So did fourteen of my family members.

From that moment, God gripped my heart. And suddenly, becoming a pastor didn't seem quite so crazy after all. I graduated from a Christian college and then went on to seminary. And today I am the lead pastor at New Life Fellowship church, confirming my strong call over the years to serve a diverse community.

New Life Fellowship is in Elmhurst—one of the poorest districts of Central Queens. And in the twenty-six years since it was founded by Pete Scazzero (who has authored a few books, including *Emotionally Healthy Spirituality*), it has influenced thousands of immigrants, young professionals, and low-income families who live in this neighborhood. I don't believe this is by accident. There are three primary reasons I believe people are drawn to us:

Theology of Place

New Life doesn't just "do church" on Sundays. Our Community Development Corp. hosts a large food and clothing pantry, a free health center for community residents to be seen by doctors or dentists, tutoring programs, community gardening projects, and other services throughout the week.

All of this activity flows out of a particular theology of place that informs our involvement in our community. I am convinced God is interested in the flourishing— the *shalom*—of a concrete place. Practically, this means our efforts to communicate God's love extend beyond Sunday gatherings. We are committed not just to the flourishing of our personal spiritual lives but also to the flourishing of our local community. One of the questions we ask ourselves on a regular basis is, "What can I do to make Elmhurst more beautiful?" I believe this is one of the reasons many people make our church their home.

Deep Discipleship

I often tell people who come to New Life to enter at their own risk. We have taken an approach to spiritual formation that looks below the surface of seeker-friendly teaching. Surprisingly, our rough and raw approach has drawn people as opposed to repelling them. I've discovered that what most people are really longing for is not a worship experience that entertains them, but a community that deeply challenges and transforms them.

For us, beneath-the-tip-of-the-iceberg discipleship means we have integrated emotional health and contemplative spirituality into our overall discipleship paradigm. We openly talk about sexuality, the impact of our families of origin, and the depth of our brokenness. We go deep in our discussions, even though they may be uncomfortable, because we want to go deep in our discipleship.

As Cate, an accountant in her early thirties, told me recently, "New Life is the most comfortable place and probably the most uncomfortable place a person can be in on a Sunday. Comfortable because I feel totally accepted as I am, and uncomfortable because in this church I am compelled to not remain as I am."

Extreme Multi-Everything

When you walk through our doors every Sunday, you will see people of more than seventy nationalities worshiping together. Yet even beyond this over-whelming racial and cultural diversity, there is a wide socioeconomic and generational spectrum. You will witness doctors and lawyers worshiping side by side with folks who are on our food and pantry line. Koreans greeting their small-group friends who are African Americans. Twentysomethings serving alongside retired folks.

On Sundays after our worship gatherings, I hang out in the lobby to connect with both newcomers and old-timers. When I ask why they started attending New Life, one oft-repeated reason is our diversity — it's the extreme multi-everything that characterizes our church. This has certainly caused tensions throughout our community (with worship style, communication differences, cultural blind spots, and so on), but overall we've found people want to be part of something larger than their own cultural norm. And when we join together, I believe we show the city what the kingdom of God looks like in its rich diversity.

I never dreamed I would grow up to be a pastor, but God surprised me. In the same way, there are countless people in New York City — and in the world — who would never dream of setting foot in a church. But they might change their minds if they began to see churches more concerned about the flourishing of the city than their own subculture and if they could experience God in a way that went beyond homogeneous community or simplistic theology. I believe God wants to surprise them. And we can join him in this work. ◆

....

Rich Villodas is the lead pastor of New Life Fellowship in Queens, NYC, where he lives with his wife, Rosie, and their four-year-old daughter, Karis. Rich is a graduate of Alliance Theological Seminary, and you can follow him on Twitter @richvillodas.

AFTER YOU READ

- What are some ways you've approached church from a more consumerist or individualist lens?

- Why do you think those lenses are so destructive to the mission of the church—to what church *could* be?

- What are some shifts you can make in your own life to order your devotions—spiritual, relational, physical, intellectual, and financial—around Jesus' call?

- What would a commitment to permanence look like for you? Does staying in one place seem possible for your life?

- What about a more intentional proximity to your church? How can you make shifts in your life to spend more time with those in your faith community?

- What might an emphasis on *practices* over beliefs look like? For you personally? For your church? How can you commit to challenging and supporting others in this?

- When have you seen the church most effectively be a "preview" into the life of the world to come?

SHARE THIS FRAME

Who else needs to know about this trend?
Here are some tools to engage with others.

SHARE THE BOOK

- Any one of your friends can sample a FRAME for FREE.
  Visit zondervan.com/ShareFrames to learn how.

- Know a ministry, church, or small group that would benefit
  from reading this FRAME? Contact your favorite bookseller, or
  visit Zondervan.com/buyframes for bulk purchasing information.

SHARE THE VIDEOS

- See videos for all 9 FRAMES on barnaframes.com and use
  the share links to post them on your social networks and share
  them with friends.

SHARE ON FACEBOOK

- Like facebook.com/barnaframes and be the first to see new
  videos, discounts, and updates from the Barna FRAMES team.

SHARE ON TWITTER

- Start following @barnaframes and stay current with the
  trends that are influencing and changing our culture.

- Join the conversation and include #barnaframes whenever
  you post a FRAMES related idea or culture-shaping trend.

SHARE ON INSTAGRAM

- Follow instagram.com/barnaframes for sharable visual
  posts and infographics that will keep you in the know.

Barna Group

ABOUT THE RESEARCH

FRAMES started with the idea that people need simple, clear ideas to live more meaningful lives in the midst of increasingly complex times. To help make sense of culture, each FRAME includes major public opinion studies conducted by Barna Group.

If you're into the details, the research behind the *Sacred Roots* FRAME included 1,086 surveys conducted among a representative sample of adults over the age of 18 living in the United States. The survey was conducted from May 10, 2013, through May 20, 2013. The sampling error for this survey is plus or minus 3 percentage points, at the 95% confidence level.

If you're really into the research details, find more at www.barnaframes.com.

ABOUT BARNA GROUP

In its thirty-year history, Barna Group has conducted more than one million interviews over the course of hundreds of studies and has become a go-to source for insights about faith and culture. Currently led by David Kinnaman, Barna Group's vision is to provide people with credible knowledge and clear thinking, enabling them to navigate a complex and changing culture. The company was started by George and Nancy Barna in 1984.

Barna Group has worked with thousands of businesses, nonprofit organizations, and churches across the country, including many Protestant and Catholic congregations and denominations. Some of its clients have included the American Bible Society, CARE, Compassion, Easter Seals, Habitat for Humanity, NBC Universal, the Salvation Army, Walden Media, the ONE Campaign, SONY, Thrivent, US AID, and World Vision.

The firm's studies are frequently used in sermons and talks. And its public opinion research is often quoted in major media outlets, such as *CNN, USA Today*, the *Wall Street Journal*, Fox News, *Chicago Tribune*, the *Huffington Post,* the *New York Times*, *Dallas Morning News*, and the *Los Angeles Times*.

Learn more about Barna Group at www.barna.org.

THANKS

Even small books take enormous effort.

First, thanks go to Jon Tyson for his beautiful work on this FRAME—offering his lessons learned (some the hard way), his profound cultural insight, and his heart for the church to create what we pray is a prophetic challenge to church life in the twenty-first century.

We are also incredibly grateful for the thoughtful contribution of Rich Villodas, who has been in the trenches offering a compelling "preview" of God's Kingdom in Queens for years.

Next, Barna Group gratefully acknowledges the efforts of the team at HarperCollins Christian Publishing, especially Chip Brown and Melinda Bouma for catching the vision from the get-go. Others at HarperCollins who have made huge contributions include Jennifer Keller, Kate Mulvaney, Mark Sheeres, and Shari Vanden Berg.

The FRAMES team at Barna Group consists of Elaina Buffon, Bill Denzel, Traci Hochmuth, Pam Jacob, Clint Jenkin, Robert Jewe, David Kinnaman, Jill Kinnaman, Elaine Klautzsch, Stephanie Smith, and Roxanne Stone. Bill and Stephanie consistently made magic out of thin air. Clint and Traci brought the research to life—along with thoughtful analysis from Ken Chitwood. And

Roxanne deserves massive credit as a shaping force on FRAMES. Amy Duty did heroic work on FRAMES designs, from cover to infographics.

Finally, others who have had a huge role in bringing FRAMES to life include Brad Abare, Justin Bell, Jean Bloom, Patrick Dodd, Grant England, Esther Fedorkevich, Josh Franer, Jane Haradine, Aly Hawkins, Kelly Hughes, Steve McBeth, Geof Morin, Jesse Oxford, Beth Shagene, and Santino Stoner.

Many thanks!

NOTES

1. "The Most Post-Christian Cities in America," http://cities
.barna.org/wp-content/uploads/2013/01/REVISED_41513_
Secular_States_Barna_Cities_Site_F4.jpg.

2. David Kinnaman, *You Lost Me: Why Young Christians Are
Leaving Church ... And Rethinking Faith* (Grand Rapids, MI:
Baker Publishing Group, 2011), 23.

3. Larry Alex Taunton, "Listening to Young Atheists: Lessons for
a Stronger Christianity," *The Atlantic*, June 6, 2013, http://www
.theatlantic.com/national/archive/2013/06/listening-to-young
-atheists-lessons-for-a-stronger-christianity/276584/.

4. Rodney Stark, *The Triumph of Christianity: How the Jesus movement became the world's largest religion* (New York: HarperCollins,
2011), 164.

5. Stark, *The Triumph of Christianity*, 164.

6. Stark, *The Triumph of Christianity*, 1.

7. Robert Briner, *Roaring Lambs: A Gentle Plan to Radically
Change Your World* (Grand Rapids, MI: Zondervan, 1995), 31.

8. Vincent Miller, *Consuming Religion: Christian Faith and Practice
in a Consumer Culture* (New York: Continuum, 2003), 59 – 60.

9. Alan Mann, *Atonement for a Sinless Society* (Carlisle, UK:
Paternoster Publishing, 2005).

10. Mike Breen, *Multiplying Missional Leaders* (Pawleys Island,
SC: 3D Ministries, 2012), Kindle edition, 2083.

11. *Manufacturing Consent: Noam Chomsky and the Media*, documentary, directed by Mark Achbar, Peter Wintonick (New York: Zeitgeist Films, 1992), DVD.

12. Dr. Fred Goodwin, host of National Public Radio's "The Infinite Mind," http://transcripts.cnn.com/TRANSCRIPTS/0108/05/sun.10.html.

13. E. B. White, *Here is New York* (New York: Harper Brothers, 1949), 26.

14. Rodney Stark, *The Rise of Christianity: A Sociologist Reconsiders History* (Princton: Princeton University Press, 1996), 82–83.

15. Eusebius, 293.

16. David Janzen, *The Intentional Christian Community Handbook: For Idealists, Hypocrites, and Wannabe Disciples of Jesus* (Brewster, MA: Paraclete Press, 2013), 31.

17. Tertullian (c. AD 160–220), *The Apology*, 39.

Share Your Thoughts

With the Author: Your comments will be forwarded to the author when you send them to *zauthor@zondervan.com*.

With Zondervan: Submit your review of this book by writing to *zreview@zondervan.com*.

Free Online Resources at
www.zondervan.com

Daily Bible Verses and Devotions: Enrich your life with daily Bible verses or devotions that help you start every morning focused on God. Visit www.zondervan.com/newsletters.

Free Email Publications: Sign up for newsletters on Christian living, academic resources, church ministry, fiction, children's resources, and more. Visit www.zondervan.com/newsletters.

Zondervan Bible Search: Find and compare Bible passages in a variety of translations at www.zondervanbiblesearch.com.

Other Benefits: Register to receive online benefits like coupons and special offers, or to participate in research.